BETTER DATING
Through Engineering
For MEN

BETTER DATING
Through Engineering
For MEN

Wendy S. Delmater
with
Brian Thies

Abyss & Apex Publishing, LLC

Better Dating through Engineering For Men
by Wendy S. Delmater (with Brian Thies)

ISBN-13: 978-0988532311
ISBN-10: 098853231X

Cover artist: Bombyx
Cover Design: Christian Delmater
Book Design: Susan H. Roddey

Published by: Abyss & Apex Publishing, LLC
Attention: Wendy S. Delmater
116 Tennyson Drive
Lexington, SC 29073
USA

www.abyssapexzine.com
abyssandapex@gmail.com

Printed by CreateSpace

To Dan,
Because Brian always wanted a son.

CONTENTS

CONTENTS (CONT'D)

ACKNOWLEDGEMENTS

THANK YOU TO ALL THE members of Wendy's dating support group on the old LJ: Melinda, Kelly, Brian, Diane, Elizabeth, Carol, Matt, Rae, Deanna and more - you know who you are. Also thank you, my dating chat buddies for your steadying influence and realtime support when it counted. Special thanks to Tom Simon for being a Canadian mensch.

A very special thank-you to family members for being so supportive of our late-in-life romance.

Finally, thanks to all the great folks at Ok!Cupid and the former personals section of Craigslist.

And to all the "failed dates"—male and female—who took the time to tell us what older people in search of a spouse nowadays were looking for.

PREFACE
by James Oshinsky, PhD

SPEAKING PROFESSIONALLY AS A PSYCHOLOGIST, as author of a book on journal writing, and as a couples counselor, I see value in this book for many singles. For starters, Wendy and Brian's writing is disarming, engaging, and humorous. Their book is a warm and easy read, as though you were hearing their experiences over coffee at the kitchen table. Their wisdom is clear and not preachy or judgmental.

While her intended audience for the original Better Dating Through Engineering might be be women, her book was perhaps even more useful as a guidebook for single men, especially for those men who wish to have honorable and open relationships with the women they date. This volume addresses the male perspective. From Wendy and Brian's more painful experiences, men can learn how to let someone down with clarity and kindness, and to accept gracefully when it is apparent that "we just want different things."

Better Dating Through Engineering for Men is a wise and funny personal narrative, told both by a strong and vulnerable woman who made finding new love a serious project and the man who would

1

not lower his standards. There is every reason to maintain hope that their success can be shared by others who read the books and follow these simple and clear suggestions for avoiding drama and sorting the gems from the jerks.

In the interests of transparency, I will tell you how I came to meet the author. I was at the time a single man, newly widowed. I was interested in re-entering the dating scene, and I was both cautious and eager. Prior to creating any dating site profiles or postings, I went to Craigslist, which I had found to be a reliable source for all other sorts of goods (so why not information about dating?)

In the "Men Seeking Women" section, I posted an ad that mentioned that I was thinking about dating again, and that I would appreciate advice from women about modern dating conventions and protocol. A few women responded as though they were early birds at a garage sale. But others offered honest anonymous advice about what women want and expect from the men they contact online and may come to meet in the real world.

Unique among those generous souls who responded was Wendy S. Delmater, who let me know that she was in the early stages of writing a book on the subject of internet dating. She shared some of the chapter drafts with me, and I offered my perspective as a man, often to say "we are not all like that."

About fifteen months went by, and Wendy's first book was finished. So, coincidentally, was her search, since she was sufficiently successful to find not just a man but a partner and a husband all in one package. I join you readers in wishing Brian and Wendy much happiness and contentment, as well as offering them gratitude for being trailblazers, leaving detailed records of the useful paths and the blind canyons they travelled on their way.

—Dr. Jim Oshinsky, Oceanside, NY 2013

James Oshinsky, Ph.D. is a clinical psychologist in private practice on Long Island in New York. He is the author of The Discovery Journal, a guided journal for adolescents, and Return to Child, a book on improvisational music making.

INTRODUCTION

ONCE UPON A TIME, a female engineer wrote a user's manual on how to meet eligible men in midlife. She understood men because she worked in a non-traditional and male dominated field, and had studied men and relationships as an engineer. She applied what she knew of engineering to make it a practical guide, full of trackable variables and continuous improvement. It worked. Middle-aged women were ecstatic. But then men started coming to her for advice...

After writing *Better Dating Through Engineering* a curious thing happened. I'd written a book on dating in midlife, which meant I was obviously an expert, right? So middle-aged men started asking me for dating help, and I started asking my husband if my advice to men was sound. He added a male perspective. Numerous men asked us to be their dating coaches, and we gave them all the same advice. So I started to write it down. They all found someone to love and thought my suggestions were helpful. Perhaps you will, too.

Guys? Let us be blunt. *This is not a book on how to get sex.* Getting sex will be a *side effect* of putting these principles in action, true, but if you're a barhopping confirmed bachelor, this guide is probably going to bore you to tears.

But if you want to remarry as an older man but you're sick of older women candidates who want to be supported while not offering anything in return? This book can help you sort out those who would use you from those who will appreciate you and enhance your later years. There are many, many worthwhile women who have been abandoned by selfish men or cads who did not appreciate them. We'll show you how to find them.

If you don't know how to talk to women, if the way ladies think is not only mysterious to you but downright incomprehensible, if you'd sometimes like to throttle some of the women in your life because they go off-topic, or if women get mad at you for no reason you can fathom, read on. If you've ever wondered why younger women can be so emotionally pliable (and boring!) and older women put up with so little (but can be so much more vibrant!) read on.

We're about to decode older ladies in simple language and give you real, practical tools for dealing with all the women in your life, whether it be your mother, your sister, your boss, your co-worker, your wife, or your girlfriend. Especially if you are looking for a middle-aged wife or girlfriend!

I'm going to give you a gal's-eye-view of what a relationship looks like, the typical ways communication breaks down, and the logical ways to solve them. We're also going to tell you how to check if any woman—no matter how hot or interesting—is worth your time: how to spot a Maneater, a Fantasy Island Girl (her fantasy, not yours!), a Manipulator, or a Daddy's Girl. We're even going to show you how to meet someone around your age who is not dysfunctional, emotionally needy, or completely gone to seed. They're out there. And there are practical, proven tips to finding her in these pages, even if you've never been lucky in love before.

Recently divorced or widowed? We're going to show you the unique pitfalls and traps that come with the territory of grieving a lost partner or relationship.

So let's get started. And do yourself a favor. Read this book straight through and do not skip to "the good parts" first. One thing builds on another here, and if you go through the book in order you'll get more out of it. The "good parts" may not be the ones you'd think they'll be! Oh, and you'll get more out of this book if you use a highlighter on things that help you, or take notes. There's a section for notes in the back.

You're holding a key to male/female relationships in your hand. There are tools to find the right spouse whatever your age! Turn the page and let's start opening some doors.

Wendy S. Delmater (Thies)
Brian C. Thies
Lexington SC, 2018

WHY REMARRY?

WHY REMARRY? GOOD QUESTION. Some marriages and divorces are so bad that the men who escape have no intention of ever getting trapped again. We've all heard the horror stories from guys who were taken to the cleaners, cheated on, abandoned, socked with overwhelming credit card debt, or lost their kids in a messy divorce. Sometimes it was the guy's fault, sometimes it was the gal: usually it was a bit of both.

Yet you're a middle aged man and you're still reading this book. You're lonely. And you have needs. You'd like to get remarried, but you don't want to get hurt again: once burned, twice shy. And you are scared of or frustrated with the search process.

To top it off, you're not as young as you used to be. Your hairline might be receding or if you still have your hair it might be going silver or gray . . . or white. You've been concentrating on your career or work and have not had time to exercise for years. Plus too many meals out and too many desserts have added up, and your weight may be worrying your physician – and you. Not to mention your knees or your heart may be showing signs of stress.

9

Even if you are in shape, there are plenty of younger men in better shape, with flatter abs, more stamina, and fewer aches and pains. You're justly proud of how healthy you are *for your age*, but feel intimidated by the competition anyhow.

Dating seems to be a pastime for the young, and you're no longer young.

So? The women that will be good mates for you at your age are not exactly spring chickens, either.

But that brings up *other* concerns. Many older women have not taken care of themselves, either, and you have trouble finding them attractive. And if you, like many older men re-entering the dating scene, tried dating a younger woman she might be physically attractive, but you worry she is only using you. Plus she's not of your generation. Cross-generational dating might be fun, but someone closer to your age will get the same cultural references, know the same songs, remember the same TV shows, and just be more comfortable to be around. Her values are more likely to mirror yours, too.

The good news is that great older women partners not only exist, but they would like to find a nice guy like you. You just need to do a little preparation on yourself, and have to know where to look.

STATISTICAL EVIDENCE ABOUT LIVING ALONE

BELIEVE IT OR NOT, your desire to find a new spouse might actually stem from a spirit of self-preservation. Maybe it's the companionship angle, or the fact that your spouse will nag you to get to a doctor when you need to, or that she tried to feed you healthy food and makes you take you vitamins. Whatever the cause, married men live longer. "Single women have mortality rates that are 50% higher than married women . . . but *single men have mortality rates that are 250% higher than married men.*[i]

Heck, men need all the help they can get in that department. Statistically, women live longer than men do – that's why although the victims of divorce are a 50/50 split, there are more widows than widowers.

Take note: that means there are lots of gals your age to choose from! You will be able to pick and choose. Seriously, that's a good thing.

STATISTICAL EVIDENCE THAT MARRIED SEX IS BETTER

BUT HEY, YOU'D NOT BE ALONE if you lived with someone, right? What's so great about marriage?

The sex.

Despite popular myth to the contrary, people in good secure marriages have better sex than those who just have casual flings or live together. They "do it" more often and are more satisfied. Makes sense when you think about it: your partner is close at hand, disease-free, and has demonstrated that they care about you to the point of putting it in writing. In front of witnesses, even.

"About 40% of married people have sex twice a week, compared to 20-25% of single and cohabitating men and women. Over 40% of married women said their sex life was emotionally and physically satisfying, compared to about 30% of single women. For men, it's 50% of married men are physically and emotionally contents versus 38% of cohabitating men." (from *The Case for Marriage: Why Married People Are Happier, Healthier, and Better off Financially*.)[ii]

WHEN DATING IS NOT RIGHT FOR YOU

WIDOWERS, HOWEVER, PLEASE TAKE NOTICE. If you have been recently widowed by a *traumatic* event, like a sudden illness or accident, you need time to grieve. In bygone days there were rules about not marrying for what was considered a decent amount of time after the death of a spouse (traditionally a year). Financial experts have a part of the reason why: they suggest you make no major decisions for two years after you are widowed. Your head may not be clear of grief, and certain things related to finances—like inheritances—take time to wend their way through the court system.

If you were widowed by a *chronic*, long-term event like an illness you may have gotten some of the grieving done in advance as you watched your wife slowly deteriorate, but the same rules apply: no major decisions for two years, and re-marrying is a major decision. And you have an additional handicap, as you may subconsciously associate marriage with *pain*. If you felt intense love for your dear departed wife, any future feelings of love may be tightly linked to painful memories of her death via cancer or some other debilitating condition. I've known men who took as many as ten years to get past that link. Even then, you'll have to be very careful to watch for ways you sabotage yourself when you meet someone you might care for.

But, to some extent, widowing is considered "honorable" compared to divorce. While stigma against divorce is less for men than for women, and the prejudice against divorced people in general is fading, it's still there – and any potential remarriage prospects may be wary of a divorced man. Plus, when is it a good time to start dating after a divorce? *After* your divorce. If you are marriage-minded I do not recommend dating while legally separated *because the decent marriageable women available at your age will frown on it.* And if separated I certainly don't suggest sex while you are still legally married for another reason, because that still qualifies as adultery and could give your ex ammo to latch onto your assets.

Here is a big thing to watch out for as a divorced man: bitterness. Hey, I hear you. I know what it's like. I was abandoned and cheated on and had to deal with his debts in a community property state. We lost our house when my first husband walked out, and my kids became fatherless. He spent my kids' money on cocaine. He even gave me a (thank God, curable) case of VD. And when I finally went back out there and dated at midlife I heard stories about how men were treated by their exes that would curl your hair *if you were bald.* So if you're thinking I have no idea what you went through, don't think that.

But to a large extent it doesn't *matter* what she did. Not if you want a new life. She's history and you cannot change the past. Look to the future. Forgive her because if you don't *she's still telling you what to do.* If you let bitterness and unforgiveness rule your life, she is still ruining your life because you are *letting* her, and you have not yet reached the grieving stage of "acceptance."

When you're still bitter about your ex, it's pretty hard to concentrate on a new gal. She will feel put off by your focusing on another woman, even though that woman is in your past. It takes time to grieve, and you're going through the five stages of grief when you're on the rebound from *any* breakup – especially a long-term one like marriage. The five stages of grief, according to the late Dr. Elisabeth Kübler-Ross[iii] are Denial, Anger, Bargaining, Depression and Acceptance. These stages take time and come in waves. It's hard not to be impatient with loneliness, but when your friends and family tell you you're not ready, they can see that you're still stuck in one of the other stages besides "acceptance."

PITFALLS AND TRAPS

MEN OFTEN SAY THEY WILL never marry again because of all the loss and pain their divorces put them through. And yet you're reading this. I'm not trying to talk you out of remarrying, and you should if you want to, but I not going to assume you've heard some of the horror stories about remarriage. People who cannot live with each other and have messy divorces are not the only pitfall. Man-eaters, Fantasy Island Girls (her fantasy, not yours!), Manipulators, and Daddy's Girls exist.

BRIAN SPEAKS:

A client related this story about a co-worker. After a whirlwind courtship, Fred (not his real name) got married and found out that his new wife owed money to just about every credit card company there was. Wanting to "make the relationship work" he chose to overlook her false declaration that she was debt-free.

Six months later, he was awarded half of her debt and she received half his property in a divorce. She then proceeded to clean out three other men in a similar fashion. (She was extremely attractive. She was also a Maneater.)

WENDY SPEAKS:

True story. Howard (not his real name) and I used to work together. The last I heard, as of two years ago he was about to get married. Now Howard and I and a couple of other coworkers were driving to a meeting in a neighboring town. Howard was driving.

"So how's married life?" I asked him innocently from the back seat. The two coworkers looked at each other in apprehension, and cast me meaningful looks. Howard's knuckles whitened as he gripped the steering wheel and his face got hard.

"She took it all," he informed me tersely. "My house, all my money, everything. She cleaned me out, six months after we were married."

Oh wow, what could you say to that? "Did you do your research?" *That would sound a little harsh this late in the game.* She didn't look like a Maneater – she was a prim older woman with short graying hair. But he hadn't researched her and he fell for a Manipulator. A quick check on the gal would have alerted him. Do your research: I'll show you how.

Then there are the younger women who are interested in older men. They want material possessions, and if you are in a position to buy them fancy things (or they think you are) you can be theirs for a season. You can be their "sugar daddy" and they will be your girlfriend. These sorts of women are legendary enough that you will probably steer clear of such Daddy's Girls but they can prey on older men and leave them devastated when the money is gone. Or maybe not money, but such females still just want to use you.

A perfect example is a widower friend of mine who was an OSHA inspector. A younger Caribbean woman who he met on vacation professed undying love for him, and he married her. What SHE wanted was not him, but an American citizenship. She left two weeks after the honeymoon.

Oh, and that Fantasy Island Girl? She is totally convinced that you are her Prince Charming, and marrying you will make her happy. In fact, making her happy is *your* job, not her responsibility. Since no one can truly be responsible for another person's happiness, you're set up for failure from the get-go.

BACKGROUND CHECKS

MORAL OF THE STORY? Looks ain't everything. When it comes to financial habits, past performance is usually indicative of future results. So I recommend a full background check on any serious prospects, as if you were an employer considering hiring her. You are hiring her, in a way; "wife" is not just a job description any more than "husband" is, but marriage is one of the most important financial decisions you will ever make. You'd be amazed what you can find out doing an online background check. Google **US Search for People Data** (http://www.ussearch.com/consumer/background-check/). Their full background check will give you her criminal record, if any, an employment record, and other financial information. All for less than a hundred dollars. Cheap at the price.

Then, if she's divorced, ask to read a copy of the divorce settlement. Yes, that's personal – but so is a relationship. You might be amazed at what it will show, or you might be reassured. You'll never know unless you ask to read it.

I also suggest looking for someone who earns what you make, plus or minus $20K a year—it can cut down on gold-digger opportunists. It's not a deal-breaker, but it's a possible indicator of compatibility.

Money issues aside, let's not forget what you are looking for emotionally. Fantasy Island Girls certainly aren't looking out for what you want! It's all about what *they* want, and expect. Older women are less likely to believe that having a man will solve all their problems, but some still harbor a Disneyfied belief that the right man will make everything better. It's easy to spot them if you ask about their ex-husbands. Everything was HIS fault. He "didn't make her happy." I'll say more about the inability of another person to make one happy in the chapter on mental illnesses. But for now, let me simply state that her saying "he didn't make me happy" is like a diamondback's warning rattle. It's a promise of poison. Don't choose a woman who expects you to *make* her happy.

Choosing the wrong woman is a hell of a lot worse than staying single. Think twice if you need sex more than you need your sanity. Don't rush into anything until you have a good grasp of who she is. You're old enough to avoid thinking solely with the "little brain," the one inside your shorts.

Unless you are rich, at middle-age if you expect the woman of your dreams to be a young, gorgeous, sexy, rich woman with no quirks you can expect something else: loneliness. If you do have assets there might then be a quick marriage followed by a very expensive divorce court.

If you ARE rich, get her to sign a carefully crafted prenuptial agreement. That way you can be as generous as you want but a prenup will limit your liability if you make a mistake. Note: define rich from HER perspective, please. In the examples above "Howard" did not consider himself well off, neither did "Fred." If she cares about you, a prenup is no big deal; if she's a predator you can find out by asking her to sign. You're middle aged? Under NO CIRCUMSTANCES should you allow anyone to walk off with the money you need to stay alive if you retire or become disabled.

Don't fall for the "if you loved me, you'd not ask for a prenup" argument. It's the oldest trick in the book. And some lawyer is just waiting for you to take her bait.

In the meantime, you're not a walking ATM. Do a credit check if you're seriously interested in a woman, and deal with the facts it unveils about her honestly.

When you read her report pretend you're advising your best friend whether or not to get involved with her. If after reading her financials you wouldn't suggest he get involved, why should you?

Think with the Big Brain. *Think*.

CHILDREN

KIDS CHANGE EVERYTHING. For one thing, issues related to kids are frequent deal-breakers for either you or her. For another, they are one of the things women might lie about at first, since they want to seem "unencumbered" to attract you.

Do you have children from a previous marriage? Does she? Are they grown or home – or back home due to life challenges?

Does she want more children? Do you? And are either of you already grandparents? Becoming an instant grandparent can make you feel prematurely old, believe you me. It's an issue.

FINANCES

ARE YOU PAYING CHILD SUPPORT, and if so how much and how long will you be paying it? In my experience one of the most difficult things for newly-divorced men to deal with is the severe lifestyle changes that come from child support being taken out of their post-tax income. You can go from a nice house with a den with a wide-screen TV, a nice car, and money to eat out... to driving an embarrassing car, while living in a rickety studio apartment with no cable and eating ramen noodles. (Hmm . . . see the section in this book on dealing with bitterness).

You can also be saddled with "maintenance" – the newish legal term for alimony. It's much rarer nowadays but it still happens, often as a tradeoff so a man can hold onto his house.

Last but not least are the one-two punch of debt and divorce lawyers. I do hope you were able to have an amicable divorce, because once one side "lawyers up" the other side *has* to, and it can get incredibly expensive. So imagine you are already dealing with any joint debt and then you incur a huge legal bill to pay off.

OH, RIGHT, SOME OF YOU don't have to imagine. You're there. And you're wondering who on earth would be interested in you as you struggle under a mountain of debt. There are things you can do. Read on.

SETTING YOUR RELATIONSHIP GOALS

DEAL-BREAKERS

HAVE YOU EVER REALLY THOUGHT about who it is you hope to meet? I'm not talking about locker room fantasies. I'm talking about your deepest needs. "Someone as unlike my ex as possible" does not answer the question – think about what you *do* want. Don't just list negatives. Make it a list of positives, too.

Okay, so what are the positive qualities you are looking for in a woman? Only you can say for sure, but I can suggest some categories to think about.

First, consider what your deal-breakers are: things that matter so much that if they are present or missing you will not consider a person. Don't settle in these areas! Unless a woman matches what you need she is not worth your time. Many people consider incompatibilities in religion or politics deal-breakers, or are passionate about hating smoking, not liking alcohol, or about their pets. But let's get more personal. You may find that women over (or under) a certain age or height do not resonate with you.

And what turns you off? Yes, I mean sexually. For Brian, light blonde hair is huge turn off and he's not ashamed of it. It's like having a favorite flavor of ice cream; it just is. When he saw a picture of someone or met someone with light blonde hair, he realized she was not his type.

What are your personal deal-breakers? Compromise on the little things because no one is perfect, but take a stand if it means something to you.

Are you retired and have all day at home, or do you work long and crazy hours? How would a woman fit into your life as it is? If you work you probably don't want a wife with no life of her own *other than you* expecting you to meet all her needs for companionship when you get home: you might not want a woman who is solely a homemaker unless she has her own interests (other than shopping!) that will make her happy. On the other hand, if you are always on the go will you have time for someone? More importantly, will she feel you have enough time to devote to making something last? It might be a deal-breaker for her.

Are you very active or sedentary? Shared active hobbies are great but if you are into NASCAR and hunting and she is into bridge club and bingo it might not be a good match. Especially if you love hunting and she is a member of PETA.

Do you have children still at home? Should she? Would you mind helping to raise another man's children and perhaps being the stepfather of her teenaged kids? Your goals will be different if you think you could no longer handle being a father or if you miss having children in your house.

Whatever your relationship goals are, write them down. These goals can change, but only as you get a better idea of whom you are seeking. Brian decided that a deal-breaker for him was "someone who was frugal." He'd had his ex run him into crushing debt, three times, and was not about to go through that again.

SOME SUGGESTED DEAL-BREAKERS:

- **HER HEALTH.** Time bombs that do not take care of themselves are not only physically repulsive, they lack a certain discipline in their whole lives. She need not be a swimsuit model, but for crying out loud at your age you might not want to nurse her until death, starting the day after your honeymoon.
- **HER FINANCIAL CONTRIBUTION.** Maybe all she can do is save you money by cooking your meals instead of you eating out, and by

doing your housekeeping for free, but *maybe* she has a pension or income of her own or *at least* she is not up to her eyeballs in debt. Perhaps you're getting close to retirement and this is a huge, looming issue for you.

- **POLITICAL VIEWS.** Not many of us can be James Carville married to Mary Matalin, a raging liberal married to a staunch ultraconservative. Compatible political views may be a deal-breaker.

- **RELIGION.** Yes, there are interfaith couples. You may not be the right person to be a part of one of those.

- **PETS.** Remember the dating movie *Must Love Dogs*? Yes, pets are very important to some people. Cats, dogs, horses and some people are great combinations. Others, not so much. Example: I love cats. I barely tolerate dogs in my house, although I am fine with visiting them at other people's homes. One older man I dated was very attached to a smelly older dog who shed constantly. Nice guy, but the whole "love me, love my dog" bit was not for me. I dated men who could not stand cats, or were allergic to them. A couple of them are still friends, but that's as far as it could go. Deal-breakers are like that.

28

OTHER DEAL-BREAKERS MAY BE as simple as certain hygiene habits or being a night person or a morning person. It might be that you like a house very hot and she likes it very cold. Maybe she loves peanut butter and the smell of it makes you nauseous. They're personal issues, things that matter to *you*.

Make a short list of your *must-have* or *must-avoid* deal-breakers. Write them down, and if an attraction occurs check the gal against your list for a quantitative analysis. How does she measure up on the things that really matter to you?

Kissin' don't last—
Good cookin' do!

Chemistry will only take you so far. Take some time to get to know a potential mate and you give it more time for these things to surface.

Wants, Not Needs.

There may be some traits in a wife you'd prefer, but are not deal-breakers. List them too, but list them separately as *wants*—things that would be nice—not *needs* (a.k.a. "deal-breakers.")

Examples:
- You may *want* a gourmet cook but will settle for someone who can cook, period. (Note: if you love to cook this might not matter to you at all!)
- You might *like* a swimsuit model but will settle for someone reasonably attractive and healthy.
- You might *like* her to be well off, but will settle for someone with a decent income and no debt, or at least a gal who is good with money and knows how to budget.
- If religion is not a deal-breaker for you, you might *like* her to be exactly the same religious or philosophical beliefs, but will settle for someone with similar beliefs: say an agnostic marrying an atheist or a Lutheran marrying a Presbyterian.
- You might want her to be a college graduate but will settle for someone intelligent and self-taught from an educated family.

OPPOSITES MAY ATTRACT, but studies show that *likes* marry. "Another crucial factor that influences the chances of a couple marrying is socioeconomic mix. If both members of a dating couple come from the same or similar background, they're substantially more likely to get married than if their backgrounds are dissimilar."[iv]

Odds are that your list of things you'd prefer in a wife will be heavily influenced by what you are comfortable with. And where deal-breakers are immovable, wants and wishes are one of the things you will find yourself changing as you start dating again. What you wanted in a younger woman, years ago, may not seem as important now that you are older. Allow yourself to learn who you are *today* and what that person wants and needs.

Write your Deal Breaker list in pen. Write your "wants" list in pencil, and make sure you have an eraser for when you need to update it.

STEPS TO READINESS

ARE YOU READY TO get out there and date? Here are some things to consider first.

PHYSICAL HEALTH

"HELLO MY NAME IS (insert name) and I am about to have a triple bypass," is not a greeting typically associated with dating success.

For middle-aged and older people, I call it the Dance of The Diseases. Will the other person last long enough for us to have a life together before one of us lands in a nursing home?

Things to watch for are pretty simple. Older people might put on a few comfortable pounds and still be pretty healthy, but--to state the obvious— dating anyone with a chronic disease is asking for trouble. Some chronic diseases are obvious, like a person with emphysema carting around an oxygen tank. Others are more subtle.

In my experience, the big-but-hidden things to watch for are diabetes, alcoholism, heart disease, and mental illness. And their associated problems.

Diabetes does not always require injectable insulin, but it still is a huge strain on a person's body. It's a fatal disease. It kills by slowly destroying many bodily functions: eyesight, ability to heal, kidney and cardiovascular functions. Diabetic neuropathy may remove sensation in hands and feet, compounding problems with healing by causing un-noticed wounds. It increases a person's risk for heart attack and stroke. Diabetic foot problems are common, and sufferers can lose a foot or even a leg.

I'm assuming you would prefer not to nurse someone through all that. She is going hope you do not have diabetes, too. If *you* have diabetes, at least get it stable. If you have a mild case of diabetes, to prepare to date you can try to get your health back with diet and exercise. People have done it. It might take a great deal of effort, but it will be worth it. Work with your doctor. Choose an exercise or sport you really like and stick with it. Cut all the sugar and white flour out of your diet.

Try using:
- *Dr. Neal Barnard's Program for Reversing Diabetes: The Scientifically Proven System for Reversing Diabetes without Drugs,*
- *Reverse Diabetes: A 12-Week Plan for Lowering Your Blood Sugar by 25%* by the editors of Reader's Digest,

- Or *Death to Diabetes -- The 6 Stages of Type 2 Diabetes Control & Reversal*

All of which are available online.

Heart issues require similar approach: a healthier diet and more exercise under a doctor's care. The risk of heart disease increases as people age: there's a greater risk of heart disease if you are a man over age 45 or a woman over age 55. If you suffer from—or are at risk for—heart disease, you should:

- Know your family history: you are at greater risk if you have a close family member who had heart disease at an early age
- Know your blood pressure and keep it under control
- Know your cholesterol and triglyceride levels and keep them under control
- Get tested for diabetes and if you have it, keep it under control because it really affects your heart
- Maintain a healthy weight
- Eat a lot of fruits and vegetables
- Exercise regularly
- Don't smoke

Heart attack, congestive heart failure, and stroke are major causes of disability. My favorite resource for avoiding or dealing with heart disease is *The South Beach Diet,* which is a weight loss program/ lifestyle change originally put together as a heart-healthy diet. It's incredibly easy, delicious, and very, very doable. Get their *South Beach Diet Good Fats, Good Carbs Guide* to make it happen.

As for exercise, pick something you love. You're not going to get out of bed to jog or go to the gym (or whatever) unless you enjoy it! I love to swim, and I love gardening; both will get me moving on an unmotivated day. Brian loves to power walk. You might enjoy golf (no motorized cart!) or love to lift weights or even enjoy lifting heavy sacks of food at a food pantry. The main thing is to keep moving and, at our age, to not overdo it.

Over one quarter of all deaths are from heart disease. If you want both yourself and your new spouse to last any length of time, this is a big one.

Alcoholism and mental illness, and their associated problems, are not so easily dealt with. In either case, you may not realize you have a problem since they attack your ability to think clearly. Here are some places to check if you are suffering from such things:

- A good "Depression Test" can be found at http://psychologytoday.tests.psychtests.com/ take_test.php?idRegTest=1308
- A test for Alcoholism: "Are you an alcoholic?"

can be found at https://www.aa.org/pages/
en_US/is-aa-for-you-twelve-questions-only-
you-can-answer

- A related (very important) test if you
have alcoholism in the family is "Are you
codependent?" http://addictionrecoverybasics.
com/are-you-codependent-quick-quiz-reveals-
codependency/
- Finally, check the "Warning signs of drug
problems" at this website: https://www.
helpguide.org/articles/addictions/drug-
abuse-and-addiction.htm

If you realize you have a problem with mental illness
or addictions, you're in no shape for someone new until
these are dealt with. Be honest with your doctor and
stop lying to yourself. Get professional help.

For a referral to a clinic that deals with mental
illness, Google these:

- National Alliance on Mental Illness (NAMI)
- by State List
- Mental Health America (MHA) - by State
List
- Non-Profits & Government. Agencies
- Self-Help Clearinghouses by State
- NIH's Institutes

Military personnel can visit: https://www.nami.org/Find-Support/Veterans-and-Active-Duty for help and referrals.

Alcoholism may be very common—one in ten people has alcoholism or is affected by it, per Alcoholics Anonymous—but it is especially insidious since it affects your ability to think. And detoxing off alcohol is very, very dangerous to do on your own: some experts say it's riskier than kicking heroin. I personally know someone who had an alcohol detox convulsion while driving, who nearly killed their son and other relatives in a car crash. *Get professional help.* For referrals to a local alcohol treatment center, call your local hospital, or check out http://www.alcoholismtreatment.org/

The same thing goes for drug addictions. All drug addictions require professional help. The online *National Substance Abuse Index* is a great place to get started on your road to wellness.

MENTAL PREPAREDNESS

REMEMBER KÜBLER-ROSS' FIVE STAGES of grief? They are important for getting over your wife dying or leaving you. In addition to allowing enough time to heal, choosing forgiveness over bitterness is essential. It can be a conscious choice. You can choose to act in ways that do not make your anger and bitterness any worse.

One of the most important concepts to grasp is that anger is very often a cover up for pain.

"...anger functions in response to a threat or some form of injustice; it is used to block off physical or emotional pain. For example, if you hit your finger with a hammer, anger is a common response. If you feel slighted or hurt as a result of someone's unkind words, you may use anger to cover your hurt since anger feels better and more powerful than hurt. It blocks the feeling of being hurt or afraid or in pain at some level. Anger also allows us to vent frustration over life's everyday difficulties and general unfairness. (From *Managing the Angry Patient, US Pharmacist.*)"[v]

So you hit your thumb with a hammer, and you get angry and curse. Why? Because it *hurts*. Men don't like to show weakness, and can socially get away with crying when a wife dies, easily. It's not so easy when you have a divorce. That's sad, because in some ways it's more painful than if your ex-wife died. There is no closure, for one thing, and she might be with someone she left you for, or find someone else later. Visitation because of children can keep the wounds of divorce from healing. There is nothing unmanly about crying when something hurts that much, but most guys seem to choose anger as a way of dealing with it.

Trust me when I say that a furious man is not an attractive one. Get past the worst of your anger before you start dating again, or you might scare away a perfectly good new mate.

ENVIRONMENTAL ISSUES

SO YOU WANT A WOMAN who can make your lonely place less lonely, your house a home. Here's an exercise to do, then. Get your coat on, if the weather requires it, and go outside your door. While standing on your doorstep get into the mindset that this is someone else's home you are about to enter, *and you are about to see it for the first time.*

Now open the door and look around. What do you see? What does it tell you about the occupant? Is this environment pristine, and it qualifies to host a photo shoot for a magazine? Probably not. Is it "lived in"? That's okay, up to a point. But if it's cluttered or dirty, you might want to do something about that.

A home or car that is in disrepair does not make a good impression. If your house or apartment could practically be submitted for an episode of *Hoarders:*

Buried Alive it might be time to clean house.

If some of the clutter in your place are the remains of your previous marriage, save a box of mementoes if you must but let the rest of them go. If your new place is smaller and there is no room to put everything, see if a relative or friend will let you store some of your old furniture for a while. You don't have to fix it all at once, but you can clean off one shelf at a time, one drawer a day or a week, one corner or box every weekend. Donate the clothes that no longer fit to charity; give away that third TV. Make your house or apartment a nice place to come home to and you might be able to bring someone new home without scaring her off. You can let her change the carpet if a relationship works out, but at first she ought to be able to at least see the floor.

The same goes for your car, sir. She is gonna see that WAY before she sees your place, right? A back seat full of stale hamburger wrappers and empty soft drink bottles is not going to win her heart. Even if your car is older, a lack of clutter, clean windows and vacuumed rugs at least allow her to hope that your home is not in danger of being condemned by the Board of Health. A car wash is not all that expensive, Windex and a coin vacuum are even cheaper.

If you are hoping to meet a gal at work, cut any clutter in your work area to a minimum. Any "cheesecake" calendars should be removed. Get one with the pet or hobby of your choice instead. You'll make a better impression with the femmes.

Financial issues

AH, FOR MANY OF YOU divorced guys the main point of being careful in selecting a new mate is to not get burned again. But if she did the same background check on you that I recommended you do on *her*, what would *your* financials say? Hmm?

You can get a free credit report once a year from each of the main credit reporting bureaus by law. Per the Federal Trade Commision, you can get them by visiting https://www.annualcreditreport.com/cra/index.jsp If you do it online you can get results instantly, as soon as they verify who you are. The three major credit reporting agencies are:

- Trans-Union
- Experian
- Equifax

(But Equifax recently lost its reputation with a huge data breach so I'd avoid them nowadays.)

If your credit was wrecked by your ex, are you trying to repair it? You should do what you can to fix it, and like so many other suggestions in this chapter you'll be better off if you do this even if you never meet Ms. Right.

Lots of the so-called credit repair companies are scams, so be careful! Some of them just get items taken off your credit report temporarily while they dispute things, and those negatives go right back on to your credit score after a short period of time once the disputes are checked out and deemed unwarranted. By then the scammers who were paid to "repair" your credit are long gone.

Debt consolidation places that offer to negotiate-down your credit card debt into a single loan at a low interest rate are a better deal. Still, check any such place with the Better Business Bureau before using them, and try to use a non-profit with a good, long track record.

If your credit is *totally* wrecked, like mine was after my divorce and subsequent bankruptcy, the first step back to normalcy is a secured credit card. I used one of Capitol One's secured credit cards to rebuild my credit. They let me have a $200 credit limit on a $200 saving account with them. They gradually allowed me to have $500 credit against that savings, then a $1,000 limit, then gave me back my deposit.

The interest rate was outrageous, but since I hardly used it, and paid it back right away, that was not an issue. As I kept a good record of small purchases paid right away (or at least minimum payments) the interest rate went down. Creditors started vying for my business again.

If you have trouble with overspending, try the workbooks and encouragement of financial guru Dave Ramsey. The guy is a riot, with people calling into his radio show to cut up their credit cards with chainsaws or in a blender on while his show is on the air, but his books are incredibly solid. He has a slight religious bent, but ignore that if it's not your thing. He's been the quickest, most reliable route to solvency for countless people. You could be one of them. See if you can find a place that runs his Financial Peace University seminars. Or take them at home, yourself.

If he's not your style, the books by personal finance guru Suze Orman are geared toward women but she has a huge male audience, too.

How to Talk to Women

The Feminine Brain vs. the Masculine Brain

IF YOU'VE EVER SUSPECTED that men just don't think like women do, you're right. Science has confirmed what men instinctively knew all along: Jane does not think like John, Mary arrives at conclusions completely differently than Marty. Please understand that I am speaking in generalities here, and that I know there is a bell curve distribution of all of these traits for both sexes. And I am not saying that men are better than women or women are better than men. I am saying that they are qualitatively different; different in ways that might not be apparent due to the ways they, as a sex and as a rule, think.

It all starts in the third trimester, the three months before a baby is born. The male brain gets bathed in testosterone in the womb, and it changes. That testosterone bath makes them trend more to being linear thinkers who focus more easily on one thing. "Scientists now know that sex hormones begin to exert their influence during development of the fetus. A recent study by Israeli researchers that

45

examined male and female brains found distinct differences in the developing fetus at just 26 weeks of pregnancy. The disparities could be seen when using an ultrasound scanner. The corpus callosum--the bridge of nerve tissue that connects the right and left sides of the brain--had a thicker measurement in female fetuses than in male fetuses." (WebMD)[vi]

Women, as you might have noticed, are not linear thinkers. "Can you stick to the point?" or "I thought we were talking about X – where'd *that* come from?" are common complaints men have regarding women's thought processes.

One way to describe the difference between the sexes' way of thinking is that men are straight-line thinkers while women are more like parallel processors. This is what causes "women's intuition" – ladies add up all sorts of things, almost subconsciously. They bring up things that they know are relevant, but are not sure why because they process them so quickly and differently. He and she may (eventually) end up with the same conclusions, but they arrive at them by different means. Neither method is wrong, but both methods are incomprehensible to the other.

Let's add another layer of difference. Men are prone to be problem solvers[vii], so when women bring up something that bothers them, men instinctively want to get to the root of the problem and offer a solution. But *what bothers women is not the same as what bothers men, since they value different things.* Women are more interested in relationships. So when you try to offer practical solutions a woman with a problem, when what she wants is to be reassured that you care or are listening, she complains that you were not listening. In reality you were listening, but not with an understanding of what women want. The solution that thrills her and leaves you looking like a hero is breathtakingly simple, once you learn a few simple tricks.

But first, let's talk about how women are "emotional."

Emotional: now there's a negatively-charged word. Please try not to use it as a synonym for *idiot, childish,* or *foolish.* You want her to love you, and love is an emotion, right? She's as much in the grip of estrogen as you are in the grip of testosterone, but guess what? That's not necessarily a bad thing for either of you once you factor it in and allow for it. The ways to allow for it may surprise you, and they are easy to implement, too.

Older women, post-menopause, may also react in an emotionally different way than younger women do. They don't have the mood swings associated with menstruation, for example.

So how do you cope with the differences between how men and women think? First, it really helps to *expect* women to think differently. Treating a woman like a man in a relationship sense is a big mistake. I suggest that—until it gets to be a habit—you consciously slow down and somehow *remind* yourself that you are talking to a woman, and she values certain things in the solutions to her problems. It will also reassure you to learn that females have (or should have) other support structures that will take care of the bulk of their emotional needs. They might be her church choir members, her fellow volunteers at a charity, her bowling team, her sisters, or her manuscript critique group.

If you do all you can to bolster those feminine emotional support systems that will take a lot of the heat off of you. But is she has no such girlfriend support system, and especially if she also starts cutting you off from your friends so you can be her world – run. She's not the one.

THE FAIRER SEX: WHAT ARE THEY THINKING?

GUYS ARE ALWAYS JOCKEYING FOR POSITION.

You guys know how it is; you sort of need to find out where you are in the hierarchy, and then move up. In a group of males it's important to know who the top dog is, and who the underdogs are, and to fight for your fair share, right? It's all about competition: whether it's all in good fun competition or dog-eat-dog, whether it's sports or office politics . . . whether it's driving in commuter traffic or proving who's better at fixing a car or who can grill a better burger - or who has the hotter wife or girlfriend.

Undercurrents of this sort of competition flow through all your relationships at work. Men never ask for advice unless they want to admit someone knows more than they do, because asking or advice is a way you show weakness (or respect). And when men give something they always expect something back.

Well, guess what? This is all your pre-natal testosterone brain-bath speaking. Women don't think that way. They've never had a testosterone brain bath; why should they?

With women, it's all about relationships.

Ladies are wired to form stable relationships. This makes perfect genetic sense, considering they conceive and care for children. So when they tell you they are upset about something that happened, usually it is because a relationship was threatened or hurt. Your competitive advice about how to "stick it to that jerk" or how to "fight for your fair share" is going to fall on her deaf ears, because her problem is probably not about competition, it's about the stability of her relationships.

And so, you get dinner conversations like this one:

"Honey, I had a bad day at work."

You perk up your ears, all ready to help and do battle for her. "What happened?"

"Betty, the admin in the next department, wanted to switch vacation days with me. They messed up in personnel and gave us both the same days!" The unspoken problem? *Betty is a good friend, and I want to deal with this is a way that does not damage that friendship.*

Ah, the helpful male thinks, I need to help her fight for what's hers. "Do you have more seniority than she does?"

Seniority? She wonders, *Why is he bringing that up? I'm worried about losing my friend!*

And it goes downhill from there, with the woman rejecting the man's practical advice about competing for vacation days. He's unaware of her core need to have stable relationships, and he gives her advice that will certainly get her the vacation days, but ruin the friendship. He gets told he is not listening. It's very frustrating and totally untrue! Of course he's listening, but he's filtering it through a male viewpoint. To her, he is totally missing the point and she gets upset when he offers his well-meaning advice. After a few conversations like this he stops even offering advice and stops listening in general.

Now I'm not suggesting you become a psychologist like Dr. Phil, but I am suggesting one of his favorite phrases, "And how's that workin' for ya?" Not well, is my guess. Misunderstandings like these can lead to fights, slamming of the bedroom door in your face, and eventually even divorce.

One of the nastier side effects of this disconnect between what women want and what men want is that men see women not competing, and confuse that with them being underdogs, wimps or fools. No, if women were playing by the same rule book as men, it might look that way. But they are not playing by the same rules for the same goals.

It's a huge mistake to apply the rules of baseball to basketball or hockey. But when you assume that women think like men, that's exactly what you're doing. Different game, different rules.

And when you single older men get out there and date, have you ever noticed that men are still trying to decide if a gal is worth getting serious about or just fun to be with, while she is already choosing the pattern for the wedding china? Women can't help it, guys. Just like you jockey for position with the guys on the team or at work, women are constantly jockeying for relationships. They are not *competing*, they are *relating*. It's what they do.

And that's why we gals can sometimes come across as emotionally needy. A particular woman may be emotionally needy, or she may not be. Jockeying for a relationship is not necessarily proof that she's emotionally needy; it might even prove she's *normal*.

Here's how to tell a potential mate is going to smother you with all that relating. Take a good look at her as a person. *Does she have a life?*

Her having a life of her own is important. It is CRITICAL to choosing a woman to marry. Here are things to look for:

Does she have hobbies? Remember how I suggested you be yourself and be enthusiastic about what you love? That goes both ways. Her time spent on her enthusiasms will leave you time for yours, unless you both love the same thing. That can be great, as long as she has *other* interests and friends, too.

Does she have a group of support girlfriends? You don't want to be the sole recipient of her need to talk and relate, now do you? Not any more than she wants to talk all day about sports and cars and guy things. In the not-too-distant past, men would retire to one room after a dinner party, and women would retire to another. If she has no one else to gab with, run for cover because if you get involved with her: tag! You're it!

THE PROBLEM YOU SHOULD NEVER SOLVE.

SO WHAT'S The Problem You Should Never Solve? A woman's assumed need to compete. She might be competitive—again, all human traits are distributed on a Bell curve—but it might be safer to assume that her need is not for competition unless she states that it is. *When a female asks you for advice do not try and solve it with practical competitive solutions unless she specifically asks for that sort of help.* What she usually wants is just to have someone else listen to how she feels, care how she feels, and be there for her. The real "problem"—her relationship need to not feel alone—can usually be solved by listening, a hug and a kiss. Keep in mind that the problem you are solving is often *her feeling alone* or *her needing to relate*, not whatever crisis or irritation she might bring up. Believe me; it avoids a lot of misunderstandings!

So now, you're clued in. And the same conversation might go like this:

"Honey, I had a bad day at work."

You perk up your ears, all ready to help and do battle for her. But then you consciously remember that she is not an instinctive competitor, she female and therefore more wired for relationships. You ask, "What happened?"

"Betty, the admin in the next department, wanted to switch vacation days with me. They messed up in personnel and gave us both the same days!" Her unspoken problem? *Betty is a good friend, and I want to deal with this is a way that does not damage that friendship.*

Ah, you—the enlightened male—thinks, perhaps she just needs me to solve her feeling alone. So you give her a simple hug.

A hug? She says to herself, *Why I married the most wonderful guy in the world!* "Thanks. It's rough out there."

And you remember that *the problem that you are solving is that she feels alone.* You decide to give her five minutes to talk about her problem, and just listen.

Later that evening you've totally forgotten about this. But (trust me) she hasn't! She makes something nice for dinner. And when you're feeling frisky she responds like you would not believe: passionate and appreciative and crazy about you.

And you make a startling discovery: listening and giving her a hug instead of showing her how to compete acted as foreplay! After a few attempts at treating her problem as a need to relate instead of a need to compete, you just may realize you're on to something good.

When you are playing by the correct rules for dealing with women, ladies are much easier to talk to, and live with.

THE FAIRER SEX AND DESIRE

MEN AND WOMEN ARE SURPRISINGLY alike in that they send mixed messages, because their minds and bodies and culture send them mixed messages. Have you ever hear the old joke that *what men want is a virgin who is also a whore*? There is a grain of truth in that.

Here is the mixed message that women send, and there is no getting around it. " 'What women want is a real dilemma,' Marta Meana, a professor of psychology said. Earlier, she showed me, as a joke, a photograph of two control panels, one representing the workings of male desire, the second, female, the first with only a simple on-off switch, the second with countless knobs. "Women want to be thrown up against a wall but not truly endangered. Women want a caveman and caring. If I had to pick an actor who embodies all the qualities, all the contradictions, it would be Denzel Washington. He communicates that kind of power and that he is a good man."

So women want a good man, a safe man, who is a caveman at heart? Most guys hear that and say, "Where do I sign up?" Not so fast. Ask yourself this question: When dating, how can I possibly come across as *both*?

Right. You see the problem.

Just as men often can be attracted to difficult women who are a challenge, women can often be attracted to the caveman side of somewhat dangerous fellows. As the old Billy Joel song says, "You may be right, I may be crazy, but I just might be a lunatic you're looking for."

So here's a little primer about having an edge, guys. I'm not suggesting that you have to buy a motorcycle or even buy a motorcycle jacket, but if you want women to be attracted to you please pay attention.

DARE TO BE YOURSELF.

NOTHING IS A BIGGER TURNOFF than a man who is trying to be someone he's not. Honestly, a guy who is enthusiastic about his stamp collection is more exciting to the right woman than an Urban Cowboy poser. Whatever you love with a passion, you should be unabashed about it. That whole notion of "*I don't care what anyone else thinks: this is who I am, take it or leave it*" is refreshing. So what if it turns a few women off? Those women were not right for you anyhow.

You get a bonus. If you are being yourself when you meet, with no apologies or fears, you get to be yourself for the rest of your life with this person. That's fun. The right woman will love your enthusiasms or at least love that you're doing something that makes you happy.

Of course, that's assuming you have a life. You do have one outside your job, right? Because a major reason women divorce men is that they are married to their jobs.

A FINAL NOTE

Incredibly, many older women do not want anything to do with sex but still want a husband to support them and will set out personals ads and profiles that make them seem like good prospects.

If your libido is dead one of these older gals might be perfect for you. But I'm guessing that's not the case.

No advice here except to look elsewhere. I just wanted to warn you that you'll run into such women dating as an older man. However odd, all of the older dating men who I interviewed found many sexless ladies like this in their search.

BRIAN SPEAKS:

Those type of women were rare, and were only interested in companionship. Typically, they were past their childbearing years. But they did exist. They did not advertise this preference, but you figured it out after a few emails.

Oddest of all in my experience was a Catholic woman who was corresponding with me. A Google search of her internet handle led me to a dating blog she'd posted on that stated she believed all men were "beasts" who "had to have sex at least once a month." She believed her church taught her that the minimum requirement, which was all she would tolerate, was once a month.

"You beast."

Right. I'm pretty sure no man would like to be thought of as a beast, and his needs as an onerous duty. So just be aware that an older woman is more likely to be honest about this preference. Just like they are about everything else regarding sex – it's amazing what older people will talk about frankly. And how sexually active they usually want to be, and are.

Our teenaged selves would have been *appalled*. Simply appalled. But, hooray for us!

THE DATING GAME

EVERYTHING HAS CHANGED.

IF YOU'RE A RETURNEE TO the dating scene after an absence of twenty or thirty years of marriage, forget most of what you knew about dating. Everything has changed.

For one thing, nowadays the average man pretty much assumes that women will sleep around, perhaps even on the first date, probably by the third and if not in three months they'll be dumped. To someone who believes in the sanctity of marriage, it's simply appalling. I suppose decades of Hollywood starlets being wooed and sleeping with the star at the end of countless movies contributed to it. Maybe it was the invention of the Pill, or perhaps it was a reaction to legal abortions. Whatever the cause, the change in our national idea of morals that started at Woodstock has turned from a subculture into a mainstream phenomenon.

And it opened the floodgates on an epidemic of sexually transmitted diseases that boggles the mind.

Epidemiology

CDC FACT SHEET | **Reported STDs in the United States**
2014 National Data for Chlamydia, Gonorrhea, and Syphilis

- Nearly 20 million new sexually transmitted infections each year in U.S.

- ~ $16 billion in health care costs

- In 2014, increases in all 3 nationally reported STDs
  - Chlamydia: 1,441,789 cases; 2.8% increase
  - Gonorrhea: 350,062 cases; 5.1% increase
  - Syphilis: 19,999 primary and secondary cases; 15.1% increase
    458 congenital cases; 27.5% increase

New and existing number of sexually transmitted infections

TOTAL: 110,197,000

Women 59,569,300   Men 50,627,400

54.1%   45.9%

Syphilis	117,000
Gonorrhea	270,000
Hepatitis B	422,000
HIV	908,000
Chlamydia	1,570,000
Trichomoniasis	3,710,000
HSV-2	24,100,000
HPV	79,100,000

- United States, 2008 (Centers for Disease Control and Prevention)

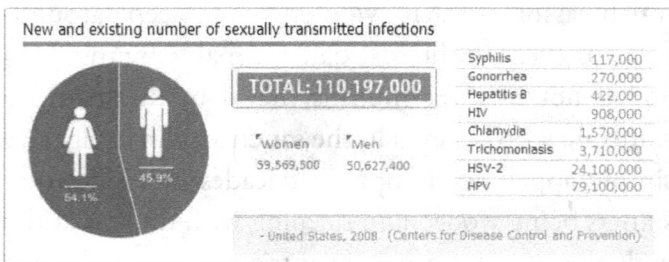

So, yes, everything has changed; it's nothing like it was twenty or thirty years ago in Dating Land.

If you're old fashioned and traditional that can be a problem. It can also be an opportunity. Why? Many older women are sick of it. If they re-enter the world of dating to look for a new spouse they can be totally overwhelmed and even horrified by the things expected of them.

If you are old fashioned and traditional and say so, to these women you'll stand out like a diamond in the mud, like a rose in a junkyard. Like water in the desert.

ONLINE DATING: PERILS, PITFALLS AND PROMISE

FINE, YOU'RE A GREAT OLDER guy and want to meet a great older gal. Where can you meet her? Dating anyone from work is kind of hard since everyone warns you about sexual harassment lawsuits. Your workplace might even have a rule against nepotism that would mean one of you has to quit if you tie the knot!

There are no singles bars for mature people, and very few venues to meet people your age. You might get lucky with meeting people at a hobby-related or sports related event, or as a volunteer. I've heard that a health club/gym is a great place to meet someone—especially at the dinner hour when married people are home, but who wants to be seen as the old guy in a sea of depressingly young people?

So where does that leave you? Looking for love online. But that opens up another whole can of worms. It's really a jungle meeting people on the net, especially considering the new cultural norms. Let me show you what to watch out for, and save you a lot of time and money and heartache.

First of all, what is online dating? It's the practice of meeting semi-blind dates via various websites dedicated to finding love. The sites all sound pretty good, but some are more effective than others in finding a decent woman to marry.

The first peril is how much this all costs. You're still reeling from an expensive divorce, and some strange woman wants you to wine her and dine her? Have you noticed how much a meal for two at a nice restaurant costs recently? Wow. Then places like Match.com and eHarmony have monthly membership fees. These can be quite steep, especially for the granddaddy of these sites – eHarmony.

Once you finally find a prospect though one of these sites, it's up to HER to respond to you, and usually she doesn't. (And what a kick in the ego that feels like.) If she does respond you may not like her profile, her picture, or much of anything about her. If you *do* like what you see, you're so out of practice that it might feel like you're in Junior High trying to get up the nerve to talk to a girl for the first time.

A few dates or months pass. You discover that the only women who are answering your ads are either so desperate, so dishonest (her photo was 20 years old!), or so self-centered that you're ready to give up on the whole thing.

But before you take a vow of celibacy, there is hope.

GETTING BACK OUT THERE

LET'S TALK ABOUT ONLINE DATING sites. *Where* you look online and *how* you look online matter. Brian and I personally researched a total of over twenty online dating sites and have anecdotal evidence of scores more.

I'm an engineer. I did a cost-benefit analysis of these online dating venues so you don't have to. Here is what we found.

WHERE TO LOOK

BELIEVE IT OR NOT, the best places to look for a mate online are free. I'm not saying that eHarmony does not work, if you can afford it, and it has worked for many of my friends. I recommend a free site: Ok!Cupid.

HOW TO LOOK.

WHAT BETTER WAY TO get your feet wet dating again than to advertise that you'd like to make a new friend? You don't have to go on a traditional date: you can meet a fellow book-lover at the library or for coffee, meet a fellow dog-lover at a local dog show, or meet a fellow gear-head at an antique auto show. Specify you want to meet a woman, and only answer the ads of those who seem to be potential friends. You are not risking actual *rejection* by a female that way. It's a great way to get back into meeting new people.

By the way, actual dates need not be "dinner and a movie' – they can be at events where shared enthusiasm for a hobby gets you together, like the above examples. Dates need not cost an entire paycheck, okay?

Take a look at the men's Ok!Cupid ads. Read them all for the past week, or the past month if you live in a less populous area. These men are your competition. Notice a few things about their ads. Are the men's ads asking for sex with no commitment – from women who are total strangers? I will bet you dollars to donuts that almost all of them are. If you are marriage-minded and honorable, imagine how you will stand out from this motley group, and in a good way. *That* should give you confidence. You will learn how to write your ad on Ok!Cupid, but you have to do something else first.

Now it's time to look at the Ok!Cupid Women's ads.

Now, let's look for trends in the ladies ads, too. What do you see? Women who say they are high maintenance, but worth it? Ladies who are looking for someone to support them? Women expecting men to buy them whatever they want because they are "entitled" somehow? A long list of requirements about who you must be or what you must look like? (And this is where all the hookers are nowadays. Seriously.) Eww. Not very enticing, is it?

Hold that thought. Now get out your Relationship Goals sheet. Anyone who might meet your goals, you can answer. If you find woman's singles ad that you like, you can and should respond, but how you email them makes all the difference. And before you do that, let's write your ad/profile for *Ok!Cupid*. Because that is going to be the template you use to answer any potential dates.

Let's set up your dating profile on Ok!Cupid, shall we? And remember, unlike other online dating sites, Ok!Cupid does not use this information to find ways to get monthly fees out of you. The first thing you see is the portal.

Go to https://www.okcupid.com/ and select you gender and sexual preference. Fill in the blanks with your age, and choose a user name and password (write these down). The next page asks for an email address, and you're in.

Then they want you to upload a photo. Please use photos that are recent and honest, and will allow your potential dates to recognize you as you are today. So what if you're not movie star material? You're you. Use a photo where you are being yourself.

Then you need to upload your profile. Here is how to write one.

Writing your personals ad

Writing a personals profile is really writing ad copy. A personals ad is an advertisement. I spent a great deal of time studying advertising, and it all boils down to some simple principles.

1. What's the benefit? The most common problem I see with personals ads is that are they are all about the advertiser. They say, *I want, I need, I'm looking for.* Dear sir, the woman reading your ad needs to know what's in it for *her.* Why should she answer you, or contact you? What problems will you solve for her? What are your features? In advertiser-speak, "What's the benefit?" I find touting features is particularly hard for women as many of us are taught to be modest and self-effacing. Men, on the other hand, need to be careful that they don't come off as boasting.

    But either way, by listing what you have to offer you are showing a potential mate what needs you can fulfill, what problems you can solve. And by thinking of the other person's needs you are setting yourself apart from the other 'advertisers.'

2.   **BE A LITTLE QUIRKY.** Some musicians think that when some of the notes are slightly off a song is more memorable. (Think of certain early Beatles songs such as "All You Need Is Love" or Hey Jude" to hear that dynamic in action, and I understand the singer Sade uses the same technique.) In a personals ad, sounding perfect does not help your case. In fact, it can get in the way.

You see, hookers are mostly no longer on street corners; they are on the internet, pretending to be women looking for a relationship and they sound perfect. Anyone who sounds too perfect is suspect, even you. Be human. Because of quirkiness, I cannot tell you how often I got the comment "You sound like a real person" on my personals ads. As opposed to sounding like a lady with her "for rent" shingle out? I took that as a compliment.

Men can be quirky by telling about their weird little hobbies, or writing their ad as if it was written by their dog, or any number of other slightly silly or unusual things. Write something like "I'm not Ronald McDonald, but I grill a mean hamburger." Or, "I hold doors open for women so feminists hate me. Am I so bad?" Or even, "I like to watch the three Stooges. Am I Curly or Moe? I'm definitely not Larry." How about, "If you know that Shoemaker-Levy 9 is not a pair of shoes and enjoyed viewing the recent conjunction of Venus and Jupiter, let's talk."

Quirky. It sure beats boring old lines like, "I like long walks on the beach, holding hands, and going to movies," doesn't it?

3. **BE HUMBLE, NOT BOASTING.** Remember looking at all of those men's ads in Craigslist's *Men Seeking Women* section? There sure was a lot of male plumage on display, wasn't there? I'm guessing that they promised everything from taking total strangers on expensive vacations (in exchange for sex), to spoiling women with massages (in exchange for sex), to taking women (whom they've *never met*) for a spin in their fancy car or boat (in exchange for eventual sex) was covered. And they take themselves so very seriously.

    Don't take yourself too seriously. If you're reading this book, you're not looking to impress a conquest; you're trying to find someone to grow old with.

So put your odd quirks or silliness or weird little habits on display, in a humorous way. My ad that started, "She cooks, she cleans, she can spit a watermelon seed further than you can," is a good example. A friend of mine who is an organic gardener used the phrase in her ad "Must not want to take all my worms fishing." Priceless.

4.   **BE BRIEF.** The main reason you write an ad like this is to start communicating with a potential mate. Too much detail in your initial response gives the woman reading it more potential reasons to put your relationship resume in the discard pile. Save a lot of the detail for future emails or the phone and even more for the "interview" (date). You up your odds that the right woman will respond if she has to *ask for more information.*

5.   **BE POSITIVE.** You get more flies with honey than with vinegar and you get more responses with positives rather than negatives. Make a list of your positive attributes, and if you find that hard ask a friendly relative or buddy to

help you. Then mention these selling points in your profile, but don't dwell on them. Instead, list the qualities you find important in a woman: values-oriented things like morals and someone who has a similar respect for hard work, or someone who loves the things that you love – whatever they may be. Birder, motor head, chef, handyman, Elvis competitor, poet, Linux geek – tell the world who you are.

Speak of any characteristics you are looking for in a constructive manner. Instead of saying, "I don't want another woman to spend me into the poor house," say you're looking someone who is *frugal*.

Instead of writing, "No hookers, married women or unmarried flings" try something like, "I'm looking for a woman with traditional values."

Instead of "No high-maintenance women need apply," make it a positive statement. "I want someone down to earth, like me," makes you not sound bitter – it makes you sound approachable.

Go ahead, write your profile. Come back when you're done.

(Seriously, the rest of the book will still be here when you get back.)

All done with your profile? Good - and remember, you can change it later if you want to. Ok!Cupid used to have huge section of nothing but quizzes, at *helloquizzy*. These were fun to do, and could be as silly as "What Harry Potter Character Are You?" to more serious quizzes about your beliefs and political views on serious topics.

What was cool about the quizzes was that if you and another person on Ok!Cupid's dating side of the site take the same quiz it automatically compared your answers with theirs, and scored how similar those answers were. It gave you a compatibility score. And the quiz section also gave you something to do when there was no one to go out with that weekend:

you could keep doing more and more quizzes so there was a better chance you had done the same one as ladies on the site. Sadly, that feature is gone.

But you can make up a quiz and put it into your ad.

Brian and I both did a lot of quizzes. We had a 94 percent compatible score. And we finish each other's sentences.

All right, we are done for the moment at Ok!Cupid. Now go back and use the info in your new Ok!Cupid profile to write that potential response to a woman's ad on Ok!Cupid or anywhere else (eHarmondy, Match.com, etc.). Don't use all of the information; try to include just enough to get her interested and responding.

You're going to sound SO much better than those losers who only want a fling.

UNTOUCHABLE TOPICS

MENTAL ILLNESS

THE EARLIER LINKS TO SITES that help you identify mental illnesses were not optional. If nothing else, they might tell you that your ex, your parent(s), your sibling(s), your old boss or your old business partner really *were* nuts: you were not imagining it. They might also have suggested you should look into to determine whether or not you have a problem. For what it's worth the new drugs for things like depression are amazing, and doctors and scientists are beginning to realize that most mental illness really is an *illness*. Like a diabetic who needs insulin, people with various mental illnesses have imbalances in neurotransmitters that can be supplied to make them well. The stigma is lifting: you are no longer treated as if mental illness is a character defect. This is good.

Maybe you're nice and healthy. If you're not, there is no reason to suffer from things like chronic, organic depression any longer. Getting problems like that under control is an important step to having a better life, with or without a new spouse.

ALCOHOLISM, COMPULSIVE GAMBLING & DRUG ABUSE

THE ALCOHOLICS ANONYMOUS, NARCOTICS ANONYMOUS, and Gamblers Anonymous checklist sites listed earlier in the book were not optional, either, for similar reasons. If nothing else doing these checklists will help you see *if a potential mate has a problem.* If you have the disease of alcoholism—and it *is* a disease, one that affects the chemistry of every cell in your body—get help. One person in ten is affected by alcoholism, either their own or that of someone they love. It's a huge problem. That also means you're not alone in dealing with it.

One thing that might surprise you is that alcoholism, compulsive gambling and drug abuse are *family* diseases – they affect all the members of a family who have not been drinking or drugging *in very profound ways*, warping your attitudes and affecting all of your relationships with impossible expectations and ineffective thinking. The main culprit is something called *codependency*. If you have a loved one with addictions, I highly recommend Al-Anon or Narc-Anon. Dealing with codependent attitudes is *critical* to having healthy new relationships.

ABUSE SURVIVORS

WERE YOU ABUSED AS A child or as a spouse? Both topics are nearly taboo, especially for men. But if they affected your life they will affect your relationships. It's best to deal with them before your past causes problems with your future. And, again, you are not alone.

The very nature of such topics makes them hard to talk about, which increases feelings of isolation. It might help you to know you are not the only one. https://www.rainn.org/get-information/statistics/sexual-assault-victims has a breakdown on just how prevalent rape is in our culture. While horrific, what's worse is most of these people as adults run around thinking that they are in some tiny, microscopically small minority. The pain festers under the surface of their lives, and never heals – messing up their ability to have normal relationships.

There is a saying, "You're only as sick as your secrets." It might be time to go to a trusted member of the clergy or a counselor at some place like the Family Service League or one of the Abuse Survivor groups at Celebrate Recovery (it's like Al-Annon, but religious) and talk about it.

Believe me, they've heard it all before.

SPOUSAL ABUSE

THIS COMES IN MANY FLAVORS. My *personal* belief is that it is spousal abuse for a wife to expect her husband to read her mind (that's codependent!) but let's talk about the most commonly defined forms.

Physical abuse is when one spouse uses physical force to control another. It's statistically much more common for the husband to physically abuse the wife, but men can be physically abused, too. Physical violence may involve a threat with a fist or object; being pushed or shoved in a way that could result in injury; being slapped, hit or beaten; being hit or attacked with an object. There may be no obvious physical injuries, or there may be bruises, cuts, broken bones, internal injuries, disfigurement, or disablement. You don't want to go through that again, as the abused or the abuser. I cannot state this strongly enough: if you are a spousal abuse survivor or abuser you need professional help. The underlying reasons you react the way you do and get into the relationships you get into need to be dealt with, or the same pattern will happen in your next marriage or relationship.

Sexual assault may be part of physical abuse. Sexual acts within a relationship should take place with consent.

Emotional abuse can include threats and intimidation, demeaning and degrading verbal and/or body language, control and isolation, subordination and humiliation. Victims can suffer a serious loss of self-esteem and experience feelings of shame, anxiety, hopelessness, depression and terror.

Financial abuse often accompanies physical abuse, or can exist on its own. A providing spouse can limit funds so the abused partner feels they cannot leave (see control and isolation, above). This is most often done by the male, but women can abuse men this way. As in the case of physical abuse the real thing at stake is power.

The other form of financial abuse is to run a spouse into the ground with wasteful and unnecessary spending. Usually this is done by the female to the male but men can do it to women, too. Problems with compulsive spending are linked to low self-esteem, and/or power struggles within a marriage. All money disagreement are ultimately about power and values: financial abuse merely takes some of those disagreements to the next level.

If Jane spends too much to *hurt* John, trying to make and stick to a budget is not going to deal with their underlying power struggles. And if you are an abused ex-husband, you—to some extent—may have allowed it in ways you are not aware of.

I called it spousal abuse, but all of these forms of abuse can be committed by a spouse, ex-spouse, a current or former common-law partner, a current or former girlfriend or boyfriend or a person in a dating relationship. The victim may think that she or he somehow provoked the abuse *but the abuser is responsible for his or her own behavior.*

Abusive relationships are a confusing mix of love, fear, dependency, intimidation, guilt and hope. There is a shared life involving family, finances and a home. Victims of such abuse usually return to their relationship many times before leaving it. Abusers may feel remorse, but feel unable to stop their behavior. Often such behavior was modeled by their birth families, and the imprinting makes the tendency to act in such a way run very deep indeed.

The first step for anyone in, or close to, an abusive relationship is to get help. In an emergency, call the police. Seek medical attention (injuries may be internal as well as external). Talk to your family doctor or community health center. Tell someone you trust, such as a friend or relative. Believe in yourself. You are not to blame.

Before looking for a new spouse, please get professional help so you can resolve these patterns before you bring them into your next relationship. Yes, this means humbling yourself as a man and asking for help. It's embarrassing, but doing the same thing in your next relationship will hurt worse.

The Final Frontier

You found her: now what?

So you think you've found a woman who is good spouse material: she has similar values and all the deal-breakers are acceptable. You have great chemistry. She's fun to be with and you think you can trust her. Great!

But wait. How long have you known her? Are you on the rebound from your divorce or the death of your spouse or a broken-up romance that did not work for you? Did you do a background check? Did you meet her family and friends? Does she have interests to keep her busy? And, most importantly, is she already happy or does she (deep down inside) expect you to MAKE her happy?

Take your time, but not too much time

On one hand older people are pretty sure of what they want and need. Really, it's one of the coolest things about being older: knowing yourself. And I'm guessing you have a better handle on what you are looking for than most older men. After all, you made out a Relationship Goals sheet and have updated it as you honed what you absolutely needed and would like.

Be aware that when you decide to marry after only a few months or a year, there will be those who will be horrified and shocked. The standard advice of "you need to know this person for at least two years" will be invoked. But you're not a 20-something or 30-something guy. You're old enough to know what you want. And you're not getting any younger.

WENDY SPEAKS:

My 50-year-old friend Jane met Peter and they married after four months, sure of who they were and what they wanted – each other. She was at a business convention and a girlfriend suggested this great guy she ought to meet. "I married him last month," was Jane's grinning response. Several years later things are just great between Jane and Peter.

Brian and I were the same way. His brother wanted us to wait two years "to be sure." But we'd done background checks and met each other's families and friends and were quite sure we wanted to marry much sooner than that.

I think part of the reason they expect you to wait is that the culture assumes you are having sex already since "everyone else is." Maybe you are. But if you're traditional and you are waiting to get married to have sex, I say why wait any longer than you need to?

PLEASE BE AWARE THAT IF you are on the rebound or in mourning, all bets are off. Don't rush into things! But also be aware that the typical man who is divorced or widowed is, if he wants to be, remarried in less than two years. That's two years max *after* he was forcibly left alone, tops, not two years after he meets the new spouse. I tell my female dating clients that those two years are the *window of opportunity* for single older men. Anything past that means he either thought he met "the one" and was mistaken, or he is not really interested in remarrying.

So no one else at our age is waiting two years to be sure. Don't feel guilty about ignoring the well-meaning "wait two years" advice from caring friends and relatives. Think with the big brain, then follow your heart.

There is an old joke that goes like this. *What do you call a 55-year-old woman who never married? A spinster. And what do you call a 55-year-old man who never married? Available.* Maybe not. Maybe you are not the marrying kind. But let me suggest that if you remarry the right older gal you will probably live longer, enjoy sex more, and be happier than if you were alone.

Marriage protects women from exploitation by legally allowing them to have rights if the marriage dissolves or if the husband dies. But be sure of who you marry: marriage also makes it easier for predatory women—and men—to rip off their spouses. Yet not all potential spouses are predators. Do a background check to reduce the risk before taking the plunge, because for the right gal the risk is worth it.

What advantages does marriage, specifically, hold for men?

If you've done your homework and are marrying a woman with a good track record, AND if you've dealt with your underlying issues like health and your background, marriage offers older men a lot. Sex without worrying about disease is a big deal of course, but, as Jeff Foxworthy famously said, "Marrying for the free sex is like buying an airline for the free peanuts." The right woman will also watch your back, make life interesting and fun, and maybe keep you out of a nursing home. Statistically, women live longer. Who would you rather have at your side in the end: a loving spouse or some underpaid nursing home attendant feeding you and caring for you when you're elderly? And remember, statistically, you'll live longer than if you're alone.

Until death do you part. A good marriage of older people can not only make the autumn and winter of your lives a better place. It can make it the best time of all.

ISO 9001 Q/A Standard
As Applied to Dating

Laugh all you want; this *is* an off-the-wall a idea. But I'm an engineer, so I tried to apply what I knew about systems that *worked*. Being an engineer is all about getting results, so I took something I knew—a quality assurance engineering process—and instead of a quality manufacturing product I tried to use it to finding a mate. *Skip this* if it bores you. What matters is that you can often take something that works in your professional life and apply it to your personal life.

- Your dating quality policy is a formal statement from you, called *Relationship Goals,* closely linked your life goals and future wife's needs.
- Your dating quality policy based on an evaluation of what you really want. To accomplish it, you work towards measurable objectives.
- You make decisions about your dating policy based on recorded data.
- As you discover more about what you really want, you regularly update your dating policy

and evaluate your actions for conformance and effectiveness.

- You maintain records that show how and where dating ads and profiles were placed, and responses were processed to allow you to more effectively identify potential mates, and weed out incompatible candidates.

- "Deal-breaker" needs determine your core relationship requirements.

- You will create systems for communicating with potential mates about who you are, what they want, expectations, dating parameters, and date feedback.

- When developing new ads and profiles, your dating plan will go through stages of development, with appropriate testing at each stage to see if it attracts the kind of woman you are looking for.

- You will regularly review your dating results through internal audits, support system inputs, and journal study during dating breaks.

- Your system deals with past dating problems and potential dating problems. It keeps records of both mistakes and the resulting decisions, and monitors the effectiveness of different approaches to solve them.

- You have formal procedures for dealing with balancing your life while dating (problems involving relatives, friends, or having a life of your own).
- Your dating system (1) makes sure you decrease the number of bad dates, (2) increase the number of good dates, (3) deals with root causes of problems in your own life, and (4) keeps records to use as a tool to improve the system.

ENDNOTES

[i] Catherine E Ross, John Mirowsky, and Karen Goldsteen, "The Impact of the Family on Health: Decade in Review," *Journal of Marriage and the Family 52* (1990).

[ii] *The Case for Marriage: Why Married People Are Happier, Healthier, and Better off Financially*, by Linda J. Waite and Maggie Gallagher http://www.psychpage.com/family/library/brwaitgalligher.html

[iii] Kübler-Ross, Dr. Elisabeth, *On Death and Dying*, Scribner, 1997

[iv] P. 16, *Why Men Marry Some Women and Not Others*, John T Molloy, Warner Books, 2003

[v] "Managing the Angry Patient" *US Pharmacist*, Berger, Dr. Bruce

[vi] http://www.webmd.com/balance/features/how-male-female-brains-differ

[vii] *Men Are from Mars, Women Are from Venus: The Classic Guide to Understanding the Opposite Sex,* Harper, 19993 pp 10-14.

[viii] Marta Meana, a professor of psychology at the University of Nevada at Las Vegas as quoted in "What Do Women Want?" by Daniel Bergner, New York Times Magazine, January 25, 2009 (online). http://www.nytimes.com/2009/01/25/magazine/25desire-t.html?pagewanted=1&_r=1

NOTES

NOTES

NOTES

NOTES

NOTES

ABOUT THE AUTHORS

WENDY S. DELMATER is the long-time editor and publisher of the Hugo-nominated Abyss & Apex Magazine of Speculative Fiction, found at abyssapexzine.com. She is also the editor of The Best of Abyss & Apex Volume 1 and 2, and writes science fiction.

Ms. Delmater used her background in safety engineering to write CONFESSIONS OF A FEMALE SAFETY ENGINEER, as well as her practical (and hilarious) guides to finding lasting love after the age of 45--for men and women--in the BETTER DATING THROUGH ENGINEERING series.

She hails from Lexington SC, where she married her webmaster and is living happily ever after.

BRIAN THIES is a senior technician and programmer with a Fortune 30 company, who loves anime, math puzzles, and various other geeky things. His book, TRUETECH, is coming out soon.

www.ingramcontent.com/pod-product-compliance
Lightning Source LLC
Chambersburg PA
CBHW050534280326
41933CB00011B/1589